KARL WIRSUM

A RETROSPECTIVE

30 APRIL - 24 MAY 1986

PHYLLIS KIND GALLERY

136 GREENE STREET NEW YORK

ACKNOWLEDGEMENTS

LENDERS
Dennis and Jean Albano
Mr. and Mrs. Steven Alpert
Mr. and Mrs. Lawrence Aronson
Don Baum
Dr. and Mrs. Peter Broido
Roger Brown
Carol Celentano
Mr. and Mrs. Douglas Cohen
Galerie Bonnier, Geneva
The George Veronda Collection
Phyllis Kind
John Koranda
Sherry and Alan Koppel
Harold and Gayle Kurtz
Robert A. Lewis
Mr. and Mrs. Terence Longo
Mr. and Mrs. Lawrence Milner
The Museum of Contemporary Art, Chicago
Mr. and Mrs. Bernard Nath
Gladys Nilsson
Mr. and Mrs. Leonard Schiller
Jeffrey Usow
Lee Wesley and Victoria Granacki
Ray Yoshida

This catalogue is partially supported by a grant from the Illinois
Arts Council, a state agency, and by the National Endowment
for the Arts.

Graphic Design: James Mulvihill, New York
Photography: William Bengtson, Chicago
Typography: Typogram, Inc., New York
Printing: Schuffelen Publishers, Cologne
Print Production: Advanced Art, New York
Printed in West Germany

Front Cover: *Boulevard Matador Star Grazing.* 1985, colored
pencil on paper, 50 x 38″

Back Cover: *Hand Me Dawn Sumi.* 1986, acrylic on canvas,
36½ x 48½″

'THE SHADOW OF YOUR SIMILE': KARL WIRSUM AND HIS ART

There is perhaps no more appropriate way of proclaiming Karl Wirsum's stature than by observing that after more than twenty years of unparalleled work, he is one of the true cult-figures left in American art. Certainly his praises have rung through the halls of officialdom on more than one occasion, but an inner-circle quality persists in clinging to the shared appreciation of his vision. One problem which attaches itself to the serious pursuit of Wirsum is the generation into which he was born. A native Chicagoan, Wirsum has long been associated with a group of colleagues known to history as the Hairy Who, artists whose late-60's debut shows at Hyde Park Art Center (under Don Baum's far-seeing auspices) caused shock-waves that still reverberate through the contemporary art world. With their temporary moniker ditched by the wayside, the (mostly) painters who made up the Hairy Who have long since gone their separate stylistic ways. Nevertheless, their careers are often seen as mutually interconnected in the public (pardon the expression) eye, and their collective genre (I will not use the I-word) is still regarded as the dominant look in Chicago. I will be suggesting in the course of the essay that Wirsum is in many ways the relentless purist of the Chicago school, and that his status as an artist's artist does not quite do him justice.

Wirsum seems to have come into this world fully-formed. His earliest extant works, painted shortly after he graduated the School of the Art Institute, are formative, but not in a way that is typical for an artist fresh out of the classroom. He is occasionally linked to certain older painters who were based at the Art Institute in the late 50's (Seymour Rosofsky, Peter Saul, et. al.), but the stylistic connection is pretty tenuous. H.C. Westermann, whose work was starting to become known by the early 60's, makes for a more cogent precursor. And of course there are his colleagues, but the core group's spring into maturation was relatively simultaneous. Yet to really isolate Wirsum's high-art lineage, one must refer back to the School of Paris, in particular Duchamp and Dubuffet. Through the former we can trace the interest in mechanization, in the objet-trouvé, and in linguistic free-association. More elusive but no less telling is Duchamp's personal mastery of enigma, heightening the viewer's interest through the lure of the inexplicable. In Wirsum we can recognize Dubuffet's interest in extreme mental states, naive and/or indigenous artforms, and in the texture of everyday existence, painstakingly recreated; the inner secret shared between Dubuffet and Wirsum probably has something to do with unity or simplicity, and the need to make art that flows unimpeded from its source.

In both Duchamp and Dubuffet we can also glimpse the source of Karl Wirsum's unparalleled wit, which may well be his most beloved (and intimidating) feature. Wirsum's eye detects mystery and revelation in the most commonplace objects and events; he sees things, quite frankly, that the rest of us are a bit too serious to catch. It is a magnan-

No Dogs Aloud. 1965, acrylic on plexiglas, 36 x 30"

Mane and Hairdress. 1969, acrylic on canvas, 48 x 34"

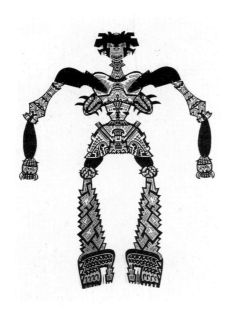

Cardbroad. 1970, crayon, marker on card-board, 72 x 46"

Cardbroad. 1970, crayon, marker on card-board, 72 x 84"

imous humor, an uncynical glee that informs the very essence of Wirsum's art. What is slightly unnerving about this humor is, first, the cosmological overtones (bliss frequently puts people off); and second, the fact that it is extracted entirely from the world which we all inhabit. Unlike the urban primitive, who imitates man in the cradle of civilization, Karl Wirsum emulates the soul and consciousness of a child.

Like most American children, Karl Wirsum wanted to be a cartoonist, a detective, a blues musician and a comedian when he grew up; unlike most American adults, he has fulfilled all of these dreams, and more. A visitor to his two-story clapboard home on Chicago's North Side is struck, first by its normalcy (the artist's two-room studio upstairs suggests a teen's study the night before the big Science Fair), and by Wirsum's impressive collection of mass-produced toys, some dating to the first years of this century. Certainly, the things made for children's play are among the most captivating objects that a society produces; but to Wirsum they are more than this. These are civilization's hidden lodes of myth and information, bearing responsibility for the conveyance of meaning from the body republic to a unique formative imagination. Toys in fact teach children to deal with fear and loneliness, stimulate their creativity, and even help them attain a degree of moral self-sufficiency. When a child claims that her doll needs love, she is seeking an outlet for emotional bonding, and thereby acknowledging (however implicitly) her own need for affection, a critical stage in development. Children *identify* with their toys, and identity is at the crux of what Wirsum's work is all about.

There is an unintended paradox in Karl Wirsum's art: he is not a naive artist, but his development has brought him closer to the folk prototype than any of his contemporaries (who frequently seem to be trying to escape its grasp). Put Wirsum on computer, have his creatures bouncing off each other in 40 million homes – *that's* folk art. But Wirsum the painter and sculptor is quintessentially modern in his transformation of the manufactured environment into high art. His popular sources often come listed in pairs: American Indian art and computer circuitry, Dick Tracy and Mexican hot rods, Persian calligraphy and street corner Santas. Dennis Adrian has noted that Wirsum's pieces encourage us "to make a specifically sculptural re-evaluation of such kinds of objects in the environment around us, things which, while anonymously produced..., are nonetheless full of the highest visual interest and surprising aesthetic potential." Although Wirsum directs one to appreciate, in particular, the mass-market designs of America between the two world wars (a period collectors have scavenged quite rapaciously in recent years), his personal range of reference is much broader, embracing video and TV imagery, baseball, the funnies, the space race and other science fiction, Hollywood, all things Spanish, the Chicago blues tradition, the Old West, organized crime, muscle-building, city parking and other car culture, and Japan. I would tend to agree with Deven Golden that Wirsum has no less direct a motive than to bring a degree of visual stimulation into our lives, "linking a myriad of fantastic, playfully exciting personages and objects with our matter-of-fact world."

Much of Wirsum's work fresh out of school was in collage, often using photos of skin diseases taken from medical texts. By the time he returned from an eye-opening trip to Mexico, his thinking about art and daily life had changed. While human aberration has always been important to Wirsum, its fusion with ribald humor in certain indigenous artforms prompted the artist to reinforce the banal with the banal, arriving at the bizarre. For example, at a Hollywood function Mickey Mantle remarked that Kim Novak's shoulders were broader than his. This double banality, a *non sequitur* uttered at a psuedo-event, became in Wirsum's mind the impetus for *Showgirls* (1969), a trio of drawings which, like *Beauty Contest Winner* (1963) and *Miss Tree* (1968), are early examples of how this dynamic functions in his depiction of goddess; built up essentially from social clichés, these ravaged madonnas are still icons of fertility, ruffled and billowing out from every fathomable crease (and then some). Wirsum makes visual and verbal ambiguities easier to sense in a series of 1965 canvasses: *Mr. Pain Close Man*'s theme originates in his curiosity about the role of police artist, but also conveys the period uncertainty over who in Chicago was enforcing the laws and who was breaking them. *No Dogs Aloud* is, like its 1968 partner, *Screamin' Jay Hawkins*, a tribute to a pair of Chicago's reigning blues heroes. The keynote painting of that year is, however, the baffling *Son of Sol Moscot*, whose composition and drawing style foreshadows the reigns of both Peter Max and Beatles' 'Yellow Submarine.' The painting's most striking feature, however, is its quirky use of double Scotch-tape dispensers to convey what the scion of New York's legendary optometrist will be wearing (or hoping to wear) in the year of Mod.

In 1980, the Museum of Contemporary Art in Chicago organized a retrospective exhibition of Wirsum's objects, an aspect of his work that dates back to the 1966 *Christ Kite*, which is just what its title implies. Because so many of Wirsum's pictures show us figures and faces as if they lie flat or in low relief, it is appropriate that he has been nearly as prodigious in object-making as in painting. *Gargoyle Gargle Oil* belongs to a series of paintings on medicine chest mirrors, and *Maxwell Swami* may be the earliest to use glitter and acrylic on plexiglas. The latter, incidentally, recalls a fortune teller at the Maxwell Street Market, while *Gargoyle* relates to a Dick Tracy character named Gargles, who strong-armed pharmacists into buying useless mouthwash. By the time Wirsum was creating such three-dimensional works as *Genuine Genie Wine* and *Schlitzy* (both derived from legendary freaks) a year or two later, his sculpture had assumed a life of its

Untitled. 1973, India ink on board, 28 x 44″

Untitled. 1973, India ink on board, 22½ x 28″

Bobbee Pin Magnet. 1971, acrylic on canvas, 48 x 38″

The Son of Sol Moscot. 1965, oil on canvas, 27⁷/₈ x 36¹⁵/₁₆″

I Am a Wall Ruse. 1969, acrylic, glitter on plexiglas, 24½ x 30″

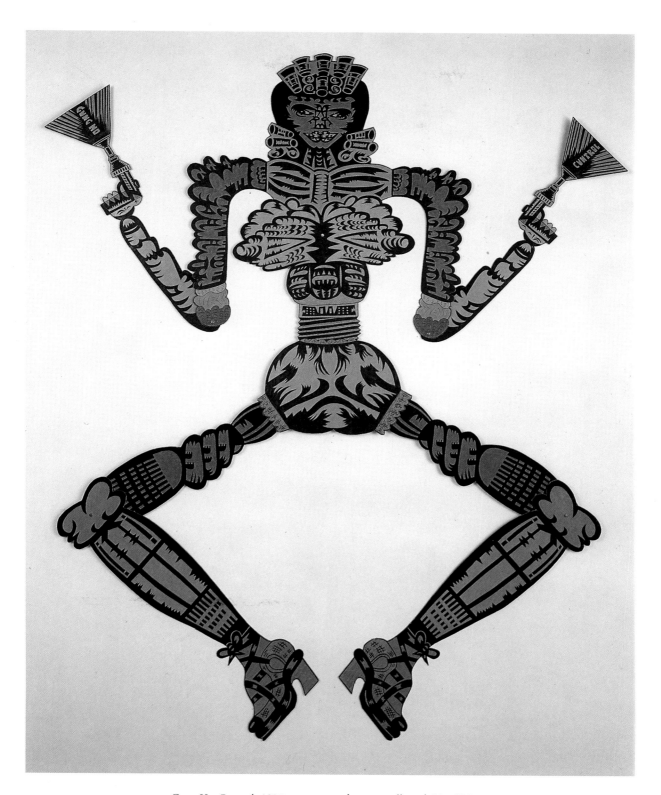

Gung Ho, Cuntrol. 1970, crayon, marker on cardboard, 58 x 55″

Draw Dick Tracy the Hard Way. 1978, offset
print, 16½ x 11⅝"

Draw Dick Tracy the Hard Way. 1978, offset
print, 16½ x 11⅝"

own. Heralding the transition is the remarkable trio of moveable cardboard sculptures, including the ferocious *Cardbroad* and the ponder-
ous *Aquadick*, who have both aged particularly well.

Wirsum's expansion into sculpture was probably fueled in part by
the so-called 'heroic' period in his painting, which is roughly between
1968 and 1974. When I say 'heroic,' I use the term non-qualitatively, to
signify a breakthrough phase in which the artist steers aside from his
contemporaries to carve out a niche of history all to himself. The colors
suddenly became much hotter, the designs more intricate, the imagery
wackier; the artist was asserting his presence with astonishing forti-
tude, revealing powers of invention and fecundity that continue to
amaze. From the lonely *Miss Tree* (1968) to the psychedelic *Bobbee Pin
Magnet* (1973), this is also the period when Wirsum's ideas may have
been strongly reinforced by ethnographic sources, from Aztec and
Himalayan patterns to the blinding graphics in the rhythm-and-blues
business. *Humid Juggler Vein* (1973), an early example of Wirsum's
series of unmounted paintings on acetate (affixed to the wall by
string), also establishes the trademark symmetry which he originated
in smaller works like 1969's *I am a Wall Ruse* (although its roots can be
seen as early as *Arm Pit Painting*). The drawings and graphics from this
period show a plethora of subjects and treatments, from the untitled
1973 ink drawings suggesting Mayan headdresses to a remarkable
group of ink and crayola studies that are unusual in the extent of abstraction in their patterning, and seem to make visible many of Wirsum's formal preoccupations of the following decade. *Skull Daze*
(1971), a lithograph, and *Remind Me to Call off the Dogs* (1973), a silkscreen, have an added significance, for Wirsum uses graphics to sum-
marize a number of iconic possibilities scattered through a whole
period's work. Finally, although the early 70's might be best exempli-
fied by watershed paintings like *Luna Tic Park* (1974) or *Wrong Faces – 7
– Same on Rye* (also 1974), I profess a weakness for less polished gems,
like *Send off for Booger Boy* (1974), a shaped drawing which, for all its
fragility (ink on rice paper), commands the wall with incredible
presence; or, *Officer Baldy Halo Copter Hair Due* (1973), from the
depths of which looms one of the more sinister physiognomies in
the Wirsum oeuvre.

Wirsum's work at midcareer (a period in which he is still quite
immersed) is a subject that future historians are going to have a field
day with. Notwithstanding some exceptions, his paintings since 1975
are noticeably less busy than their predecessors, but individual images
are richer, more harmonically composed, and each seems to convey a
broader range of meanings. These forms are, in a way, emblems of
experience, and the background information applicable to each enliv-
ens the process of interpretation considerably. The famous *Parking*
series from 75-76 – including *Parking Attendance is Up, Park A Lot* and
Parking Attendants Attend Dance – is based upon Wirsum's observa-

tions of the car jocks employed by a stadium, who are giving a lively gestural performance. *Hari Kari's Arms Exchange* (1976) was inspired by news reports of the discovery of aged Japanese servicemen who hadn't known World War II was over; and by the name Harry Carey, a sports announcer at the time the Chicago White Sox were sold. The *Great Skates* series (1976) relates, in part, to information about how specialized repetitious activity has a tendency to overdevelop certain parts of the human physique. This group is one of the earliest in which can be seen Wirsum's treatment of characters who seem to be passing through the picture-plane on their way to someplace else. This can be witnessed in such recent paintings as *Mr. Whatzit on the Road to Burma-Shave* or *Boulevard Matador Star Grazing* (both 1985), in contrast to the stock-still frontal orientation of the figures in *3 My Eye Land Cyclops* or *Bone of Contention* (both 1983).

By taking facts as auspicious suggestions, Wirsum is deliberately seeking to superimpose a semi-metaphysical grid over a series of accidental occurrences. This pre-rational orientation has its mystical side, of course, to counter the absurdist thrust of the artist's cosmology. 1978's *Sand Blast Distributing Co.*, which shows someone reading a non-existent newspaper in space, was inspired by speculation about whether an escaped Macy's float would, in fact, enter the Earth's orbit. *Planting Planters Interceding* (1978) has a related 'science' angle, as it depicts a pair of people-implants, such as might have been left in Earth millions of years ago by passing aliens looking to colonize. We share with the artist our knowledge that these things are somehow too marginal for all the attention he is giving them, yet he still convinces us that he's onto something (revelatory, that is). The guiltiest pleasures for a Wirsum fan are probably those works which are so hopelessly charming that they almost look subversive. I refer, of course, to the mice and bunny pieces, which at points seem to have crowded all other subjects out of the studio (Wirsum shrugs and explains that if he were going to make rodents at all, naturally he felt that he ought to make lots of them . . .) These works are in fact quite baffling, even frustrating to the extent that they are so blatantly the work of a happy man, and happy is simply not an art-historical classification. The mice and bunnies can be found nearly anytime, but they predominate in the 80's. The *Count Fasco's Mouse Piece* series, outlined white on white with red highlights, is extraordinarily droll even for Wirsum. Less austere are *Public Squeaker #1* and *Rabbit Rat Blown up out of Proportion* (combining the artist's two pet themes), both painted in 1982 with a peel-off glossiness. Just as most of Wirsum's people have animal characteristics, so his critters are at least part-human. The *'Pig Women'* series, which includes *I'm a Lonely Little Petunia Tip-Toeing through an Onion Patch* and the unforgettable *Mind Your P's and Q's* (both '82), is a good example of the metamorphosis which seems to be happening in Wirsum's characters as we watch. Overflowing with oddnesses and

Draw Dick Tracy the Hard Way. 1978, offset print, 16½ x 11⅝″

Draw Dick Tracy the Hard Way. 1978, offset print, 16½ x 11⅝″

Double Dribble in the Ozone. 1985, acrylic on canvas, 52½ x 43½"

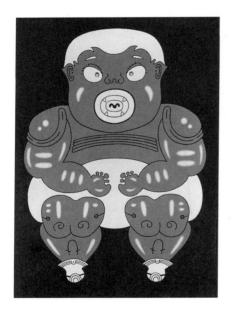

Stork Reality. 1985, acrylic on canvas, 32½ x 23½"

quirks, they are nonetheless inextricably bonded to the human spirit, if chiefly through their bathos. *Snow Crows Tip Their Hats* always makes me catch my breath, for it has vague antecedents somewhere in a long-forgotten TV commercial from my childhood; through its transformation, it is twice a visitor: once from past to present, and second, from the world of empty sentiment to the world of high beauty.

For Karl Wirsum, each image has its own genesis; if it is a painting, then it exists as a drawing, too; but if it is a drawing, then it might result in a painting, three paintings, or it might just stay a drawing. *Boulevard Matador Star Grazing* (1985) is a particularly strong example of a drawing as captivating as – and with the physical presence of – a canvas. The complex background suggests work from the early 70's, although the pose is clearly of the more recent 'strolling-through' genre. With his suspended elbows and elevated heels, this matador recalls another remarkable character, *Redfinger Girl* (1981), a second cousin to John Dillinger's Lady in Red. As these two exit stage right, the hero of *Spitting Image* (1981) squirts green saliva through twin tooth-gaps, aiming in the general vicinity of the viewer's right shoe. Another distortion technique in recent Wirsum is the anamorphism that slips into paintings like *Koranda Approaching the Veranda* (1983), and the shimmering acetate creation, *Coma Dent* (1985), both heightened in complexity through the sidelong attenuation of the figures. Wirsum currently seems to be exploring compositions which not only embrace asymmetry, but even align themselves predominantly off-center. *Bad Mitten Citizen* (1984) and *Duck's Breath Lays an Egg* (1985) are two variations on off-centeredness that may indicate a few impending changes in Wirsum's style. In form and execution they recall certain of the earliest black paintings, *Into Each Life a Little Rain Must Spring* or *Wishbone Shadow* (both from '79), but they also experiment with the deployment of curious object-forms which seem to be occurring with greater frequency in Wirsum's recent work. Sometimes these prop/ornaments are easily-identified – in *Badmitten* and *Duck's Breath*, and also in *Double Dribble in the Ozone* (1985) and *Heads I Lose, Tails you Win* (1986). In the disarming *Mr. Whatzit on the Road to Burma-Shave*, however, or the loveable *Tramp Alien*, (both 1985) these references are unsettlingly oblique both in appearance and intent.

Perhaps some of this current activity points to a budding interest in naturalism for Wirsum, which would shed some light on the increasingly precious nature of his cut-out and three-dimensional work. The vulnerability we can detect in the *Assorted Window Silly Series – Bunny Model .0052* or *Fido, Ray and Me* (1985) is the plastic equivalent of the strange directness found in the self-portrait *Me* (1985), or in *Leave Your Smell on Earth* (1984), which commemorates a friend's deathbed dream. I wonder if Wirsum is not indirectly addressing the current object-fetishization in the art world, with our lust for oversized histrionic paintings, and how this lack of self-consciousness is beginning to

Skull Daze. 1971, silkscreen, 24 x 34″ (Edition of 50)

Me. 1985, acrylic on canvas, 52½ x 36″

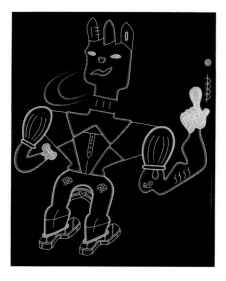

The Arched Flip: Heads I Lose, Tails You Win. 1986, acrylic on canvas, 50½ x 40¼″

numb our aesthetic sensitivity. There is something so perishable about *Wrinkled Rabbit* or even the comparatively indestructible *Brown Derby Bouncer* or *Robert Bounce or Fly* (both 1983), that if we permit this work to do more than charm us, we are forced to confront our own temporality, not to mention certain of our collective expectations about what constitutes important and serious art.

Despite these thoughts about a more somber subtext in recent Wirsum, I would like to close by making a case for his work's importance by virtue of its compelling serenity, a quality normally associated with such abstract mavericks as John McLaughlin or Myron Stout. Through its inexhaustible meditations on the body as a system, in its painstaking care to be always enigmatic but never aloof, and by the grace with which it throws a modern lifeline to archaic modes of life and thought, Wirsum's art is at once both intimate and profound. Its perfect equilibrium is simultaneously a refinement of and an antidote to a culture of material distractions. Despite (or because of) its unquenchable humor, this work has managed to project an honesty that affects us deeply without our complete awareness of its full significance. Yet my guess is that even this little secret about Karl Wirsum and his art will not be a secret much longer. The range and depth of these two decades' worth of paintings, drawings, objects and sculpture should establish that Wirsum is immeasurably more than a fringe sensibility, and may even project him into that improbable role which he most deserves – an American master.

DAN CAMERON
New York, Winter 1986

Installation Views: Museum of Contemporary Art, Chicago   2 December 1980 - 22 February 1981

Great Skates #1. 1976, acrylic on board, 41½ x 31½"

Mr. Big Arms in a No Swipe Place. 1977, acrylic on acetate, 28 x 23"

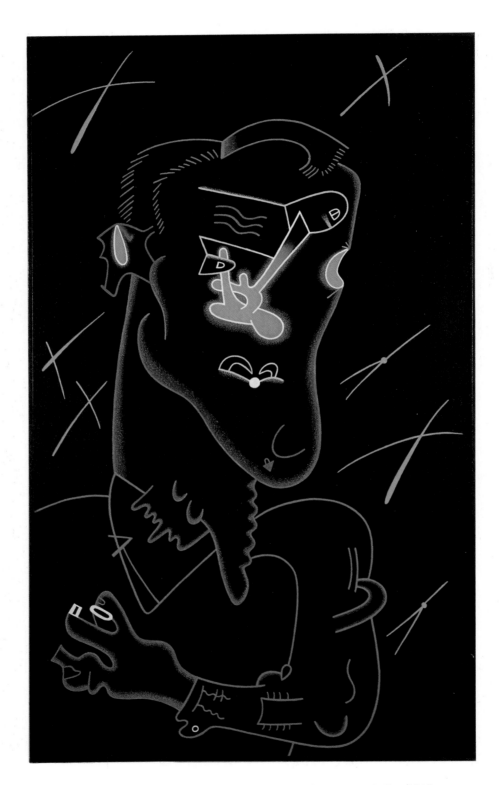

Into Each Life a Little Rain Must Spring. 1979, acrylic on canvas, 38½ x 21½″

Red Finger Girl (Biographic Biography). 1981, crayon on paper, 29⅞ x 22½″

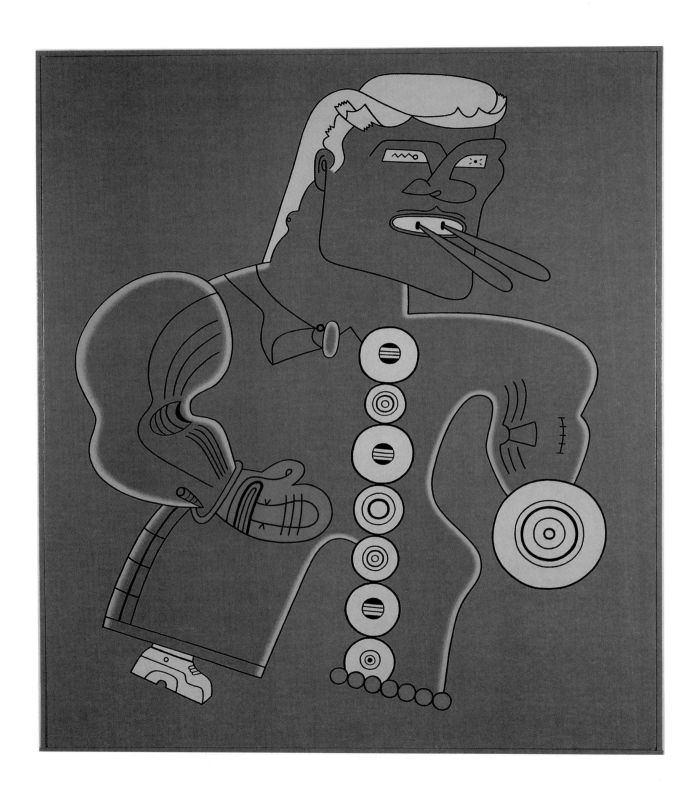

Spitting Image. 1983, acrylic on canvas, 33½ x 28½″

Mind Your P's & Q's. 1982, acrylic on canvas, 43½ x 25½″

Brown Derby Bouncer. 1983, acrylic on wood, 45 x 31 x 7¾"

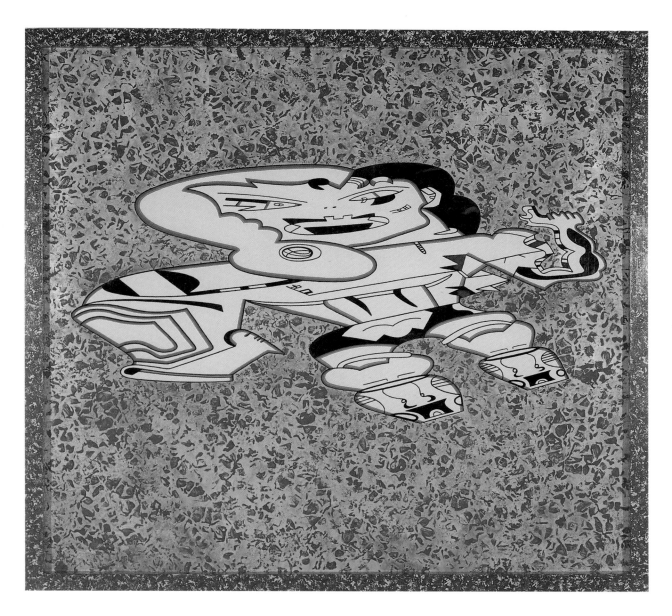

Coma Dent. 1985, acrylic on acetate, 42 x 44½"

Tuskarama Nails One Down. 1986, acrylic on canvas, 50½ x 36½″

BIOGRAPHY

BORN: 1939, Chicago, Illinois

RESIDENCE: Chicago

EDUCATION: The School of the Art Institute of Chicago, B.A.

SELECTED PUBLIC COLLECTIONS
Whitney Museum of American Art, New York
National Museum of American Art, Smithsonian Institution,
Washington, D.C.
The Art Institute of Chicago
Museum des 20. Jahrhunderts, Vienna
Museum of Contemporary Art, Chicago
Kalamazoo Institute of Art, Michigan
Krannert Art Museum, University of Illinois, Champaign
David and Alfred Smart Gallery, University of Chicago
The Illinois Collection for the State of Illinois Center, Chicago
American Telephone & Telegraph, New York
Ball State University, Muncie, Indiana
First National Bank of Chicago
Weatherspoon Art Gallery, University of N.C., Greensboro
Chase Manhattan Bank, New York

ONE-PERSON EXHIBITIONS
1986   Phyllis Kind Gallery, New York
1984   Phyllis Kind Gallery, Chicago
1983   Phyllis Kind Gallery, New York
1982   Phyllis Kind Gallery, Chicago
        Southeastern Center for Contemporary Art,
        Winston-Salem, North Carolina
1981   Phyllis Kind Gallery, Chicago
        'Hare Toddy Kong Tamari: Objects Selected by Karl
        Wirsum', Museum of Contemporary Art, Chicago
1980   Phyllis Kind Gallery, Chicago
1979   Phyllis Kind Gallery, New York
1978   Phyllis Kind Gallery, Chicago
1977   Phyllis Kind Gallery, New York
1976   Phyllis Kind Gallery, Chicago
1974   Phyllis Kind Gallery, New York
1971   Wabash Transit Gallery, Chicago
1970   St. Xavier College, Chicago
1967   Dell Gallery, Chicago

SELECTED GROUP EXHIBITIONS
1986   Komic Ikonoclasm. ICA Gallery, London, England and
        traveling exhibition
1985-86   Correspondences: New York Art Now. Laforet
        Museum, Tokyo, Japan and traveling exhibition
1985   Modern Masks. The Whitney Museum of American Art
        at Philip Morris, New York
        Wood Hue or Knot? Sculpture Exhibition, Phyllis Kind
        Gallery, Chicago
1984   Visions of Childhood: A Contemporary Iconography.
        Whitney Museum of American Art at Federal Hall,
        New York
        80th Exhibition by Artists of Chicago and Vicinity. The
        Art Institute of Chicago
        10 Years of Collecting at the MCA. Museum of
        Contemporary Art, Chicago
        Chicago Cross-Section. Trisolini Gallery, University of

Ohio at Athens
        Chicago Imagist Update. Phyllis Kind Gallery, Chicago
1983   Gladys Nilsson, Jim Nutt, Ed Paschke, Suellen Rocca,
        Karl Wirsum. Galerie Bonnier, Geneva, Switzerland
        The Comic Art Show. Whitney Museum of American
        Art at Federal Hall, New York
        The Last Laugh. Southern Ohio Museum and Cultural
        Center, Portsmouth and traveling exhibition
        The Big Pitcher Show: 20 Years of the Abstracted Figure in
        Chicago Art. Hyde Park Art Center, Chicago
1982   Painting and Sculpture Today: 1982. Indianapolis
        Museum of Art, Indiana
        Chicago on Paper. Ray Hughes Gallery, Brisbane,
        Australia
        From Chicago. Pace Gallery, New York
        Selections from the Dennis Adrian Collection. Museum of
        Contemporary Art, Chicago
1980-82   Who Chicago? An Exhibition of Contemporary
        Imagists. Sunderland Arts Centre Sunderland, England
        and traveling show (Camden Arts Centre, Glasgow;
        The National Museum of Modern Art, Edinburgh;
        Glynvivian Gallery, Swansea, Wales; The Institute of
        Contemporary Art, Boston; Contemporary Arts
        Center, New Orleans)
1981   Figuratively Sculpting. Institute for Art and Urban
        Resources at P.S. 1, Long Island City, New York
        New Dimensions in Drawing. The Aldrich Museum,
        Ridgefield, Connecticut
        The Broken Surface. Bennington College, Vermont;
        Tibor de Nagy Gallery, New York; Virginia Technical
        College, Blacksburg, Virginia
1980   Contemporary Drawings and Watercolors. Memorial Art
        Gallery of the University of Rochester, New York
        Six Artists from Chicago. The Mayor Gallery, London
        Some Recent Art from Chicago. The Ackland Museum of
        Art, University of North Carolina at Chapel Hill
1979   Art Inc. - American Paintings from Corporate Collections.
        Montgomery Museum of Fine Art, Alabama; Corcoran
        Gallery of Art, Washington, D.C.; Indianapolis
        Museum of Art, Indiana; San Diego Museum of Art,
        California
        Chicago Currents: The Koffler Foundation. The National
        Collection of Fine Arts, Washington, D.C.
        Material Pleasures. Institute of Contemporary Art,
        University of Pennsylvania, Philadelphia
1978   Contemporary Chicago Painters. University of Northern
        Iowa Gallery of Art, Ceder Rapids
        Eleven Chicago Painters. University of Southern Florida,
        Gallery of Art, Tallahassee
1977   Masterpieces of Chicago Art. Chicago Public Library
        Cultural Center, Illinois
        The Chicago Connection. E.B. Crocker Art Gallery,
        Sacramento and traveling exhibition
1974   75th Exhibition by Artists of Chicago and Vicinity. The
        Art Institute of Chicago
1973-74   XII Biennal de Sao Paulo. Sao Paulo, Brazil and
        traveling exhibition throughout South America (an
        enlarged exhibition, Made in Chicago, was installed at
        The National Collection of Fine Arts, Smithsonian
        Institution, Washington, D.C. and at the The Museum

BIBLIOGRAPHY

BOOKS AND CATALOGUES

Ackland Art Museum, University of North Carolina. *Some Recent Art from Chicago.* Chapel Hill: The Ackland Art Museum, 1980. Introduction by Katherine Lee Keefe.

Ceolfrith Gallery, Sunderland Arts Centre. *Who Chicago? An Exhibition of Contemporary Imagists.* Sunderland, Tyne and Wear, England: Sunderland Arts Centre, 1981. Preface by Tony Knipe. Introduction by Victor Musgrave. Essays by Dennis Adrian, Russell Bowman and Roger Brown.

Florida State University Gallery. *Eleven Chicago Painters.* Tallahasee: Florida State University Gallery, 1978. Introduction by Sanford Sivitz Shaman. Essay by Margaret Miller.

Galerie Bonnier. *Gladys Nilsson, Jim Nutt, Ed Paschke, Suellen Rocca, Karl Wirsum.* Geneva: Galerie Bonnier, 1983.

Illinois Arts Council. *Koffler Foundation Collection.* Chicago: Illinois Arts Council, 1976. Essay by Dennis Adrian.

Institute of Contemporary Art. *Material Pleasures/The Fabric Workshop at ICA.* Philadelphia: ICA, University of Pennsylvania, 1979. Introduction by Michael Quigley.

Lucie-Smith, Edward. *American Art Now.* New York: William Morrow and Company, 1985. pp. 122, 124.

Lucie-Smith, Edward. *Cultural Calendar of the 20th Century.* Oxford: Phaidon Press Limited, 1979. p. 145.

Madison Art Center. *Contemporary Figurative Painting in the Midwest.* Madison: University of Wisconsin, 1977.

The Mayor Gallery. *Sculpture Then and Now.* London: The Mayor Gallery, 1983.

Montgomery Museum of Fine Arts. *American Painting of the Sixties and Seventies: The Real / The Ideal / The Fantastic.* Montgomery: Montgomery Museum of Fine Arts, 1980. pp. 58, 59, 60, 61, 70, 83. Essay by Mitchell Kahan.

Montgomery Museum of Fine Arts. *Art Inc.: American Paintings from Corporate Collections.* Montgomery: Montgomery Museum of Fine Arts in association with Brandywine Press, 1979. Edited and with an introduction by Mitchell Douglas Kahan.

Museum of Contemporary Art. *Hare Toddy Kong Tamari: Objects Selected by Karl Wirsum.* Chicago: Museum of Contemporary Art, 1980. Essay by Dennis Adrian.

Museum of Contemporary Art. *Selections from the Dennis Adrian Collection.* Chicago: Museum of Contemporary Art, 1982. pp. 4, 7, 45-46. Introduction by John Hallmark Neff. Essay by Dennis Adrian. Texts by Mary Jane Jacob, Lynn Warren and Naomi Vine.

Museum of Contemporary Art. *Made in Chicago: Some Resources.* Chicago: Museum of Contemporary Art, 1975. Introduction by Don Baum.

Museum of Contemporary Art. *Pictures to Be Read/Poetry to Be Seen.* Chicago: Museum of Contemporary Art, 1968. Essay by Don Baum and Stephen Prokopoff.

National Collection of Fine Arts. *Made in Chicago.* Washington, DC: Smithsonian Institution Press, 1974. Essays by Whitney Halstead and Dennis Adrian.

The Pace Gallery. *From Chicago.* New York: Pace Gallery Publications, 1981. Essay by Russell Bowman.

Schulze, Franz. *Fantastic Images: Chicago Art Since 1945.* Chicago: Follett Publishing Company, 1972. pp. 6, 7, 29, 31, 33, 34, 38, 160-161, 180-187.

Southeastern Center for Contemporary Art, Wake Forest University. *Karl Wirsum.* Winston/Salem: Southeastern Center for Contemporary Art, 1982.

University of Northern Iowa Gallery of Art. *Contemporary Chicago Painters.* Cedar Falls: Gallery of Art, Department of Art, University of Northern Iowa, 1978. Introduction and Texts by Sanford Sivitz Shaman.

University of Michigan Museum of Art. *Chicago: The City and Its Artists 1945-1978.* Ann Arbor: University of Michigan Museum of Art, 1978.

University of Pennsylvania. *The Spirit of the Comics.* Philadelphia: University of Pennsylvania, 1969. Essay by Joan C. Siegfried.

Whitney Museum of American Art. *Human Concern/Personal Torment.* New York: Whitney Museum of American Art, 1969. Essay by Robert C. Doty.

ARTICLES AND REVIEWS

Adrian, Dennis, 'Karl Wirsum.' *Arts,* vol. 54 no. 3 (November 1979). p. 6.

Adrian, Dennis. 'The Inventive Karl Wirsum.' *Chicago Daily News,* Thursday, June 13, 1974. p. 40.

Adrian, Dennis. 'Drawing in Chicago: The Second Wave.' *Drawing,* vol. IV no. 5 (January-February 1983). pp. 105-107.

Adrian, Dennis. 'Aspects of Form Among Some Chicago Artists.' *Art Scene,* vol. 2 no. 7 (April 1969). pp. 10-15.

Artner, Alan. 'Art/Exhibit's Title Unwittingly Accurate.' *Chicago Tribune,* Friday, January 2, 1981.

Gedo, Mary Matthews. 'Interconnections: A Study of Chicago Style Relationships in Painting.' *Arts,* vol. 58 no. 1 (September 1983). pp. 92-97.

Golden, Deven K. 'Karl Wirsum.' *New Art Examiner,* (Summer 1984).

Januszcak, Waldemar. 'Chicago Defies You to Like its Art.' *The Arts Guardian* (London), Wednesday, December 17, 1980.

Kirschner, Judith Russi. 'Chicago: Karl Wirsum.' *Artforum,* vol. XXIII, (October 1984). pp. 95-96.

Kozloff, Max. 'Inwardness: Chicago Art Since 1945.' *Artforum,* vol. 11 no. 2 (October 1972). pp. 51-55.

Lubell, Ellen, 'Arts Reviews / Karl Wirsum.' *Arts,* vol. 51 no. 9 (May 1977). pp. 38-39.

Lyon, Christopher. 'Karl Wirsum.' *New Art Examiner,* (Summer 1981).

Perrault, John. 'Second City: Second Thoughts.' *The Soho News,* February 16, 1982. p. 56.

Rickey, Carrie. 'Art: The Midwest, A Special Report / Chicago.' *Art in America,* vol. 67 no. 4 (July-August 1979). pp. 47-56.

Russell, John. 'The Hairy Who and Other Messages from Chicago.' *New York Times,* Sunday, January 31, 1982. p. 29.

Schjeldahl, Peter. 'Letter from Chicago.' *Art in America,* vol. 64 no. 4 (July-August 1976). pp. 52-58.

Schulze, Franz. 'Artnews in Chicago.' *Art News,* vol. 70 no. 7 (November 1971). pp. 51-53.

Schulze, Franz. 'Made in Chicago: A Revisionary View.' *Art in America,* vol. 71 no. 3 (March 1983). pp. 122-128.

Shepherd, Michael. 'Chicago, Chicago....' *Arts Review of Great Britain,* vol. XXXI no. 12, Friday, June 22, 1979. p. 315.

Upshaw, Reagan. 'Painting in Chicago: Blue Collar Surrealism Meets Prairie Abstraction.' *Portfolio,* vol. IV no. 3 (May-June 1982). pp. 56-63.

CATALOGUE OF THE EXHIBITION

1) *Mr. Pain Close Man.*   1965
Oil on canvas, 30 x 18″
Collection: Phyllis Kind

2) *No Dogs Aloud.*   1965
Acrylic on plexiglas, 36 x 30″
Collection: Don Baum

3) *The Son of Sol Moscot.*   1965
Oil on canvas, 27⅞ x 36¹⁵⁄₁₆″
Private Collection

4) *Armpits.*   1965
Acrylic and fur on canvas, 28 x 26″
Collection: Mr. and Mrs. Lawrence Aronson

5) *Genuine Genie Wine.*   1967
Acrylic on paper maché, 36″ high
Collection: Ray Yoshida

6) *Gila Teen.*   1968
Acrylic on canvas, 24 x 21″
Collection: Gladys Nilsson

7) *Showgirl #3.*   1969
Acrylic on canvas, 26 x 39″
Collection: John Koranda

8) *I Am a Wall Ruse.*   1969
Acrylic, glitter on plexiglas, 24½ x 30″
Private Collection

9) *Aquadick.*   1970
Ink, crayon, marker on cardboard, 60 x 55″
Collection: Mr. and Mrs. Lawrence Aronson

10) *Gung Ho Cuntrol.*   1970
Ink, crayon, marker on cardboard, 58 x 55″

11) *Teresa's Torso #1.*   1970-71
Ink, crayon on cardboard, 40 x 30″

12) *Teresa's Torso #2.*   1970-71
Ink, crayon on cardboard, 40 x 30″

13) *Skull Daze.*   1971
Silkscreen, 24 x 34″ (Edition of 50)

14) *Chest Peter.*   1971
Acrylic on wood, 36 x 18 x 7″
Collection: Mr. and Mrs. Bernard Nath

15) *Untitled.*   1973
India ink on paper, 22½ x 28″

16) *Untitled.*   1973
India ink on paper, 40 x 30″

17) *Bobbee Pin Magnet.*   1973
Acrylic on canvas, 48 x 38″
The George Veronda Collection

18) *Humid Juggler Vein.*   1971
Acrylic on acetate, 42½ x 32¾″
Collection: Dr. and Mrs. Peter Broido

19) *Double Might Twine.*   1973-74
Acrylic on wood, satin clothes, 40″ high
Collection of the artist

20) *Double Mite Twine.*   1973-74

Acrylic on wood, satin clothes, 40″ high
Collection of the artist

21) *Lollipup.* 1973-74
Acrylic on wood, 18″ high
Collection of the artist

22) *Pinsetter.* 1973-74
Acrylic on wood, 40½″ high
Collection: Sherry and Alan Koppel

23) *Sim Blattner.* 1973-74
Acrylic on wood, 38¾ x 13½ x 5″
Collection: Dennis and Jean Albano

24) *Korner Kite.* 1974
Colored ink on rice paper, 29½ x 23¼″

25) *Send-Off for Booger Boy Comic Strip*
by Fosher. (Kite) 1974
India ink on rice paper, 44½ x 32¾″

26) *Untitled.* (Kite) 1974
Colored ink on rice paper, 46½ x 30″

27) *Remind Me to Call Off the Dogs.* 1974
Silkscreen, 29 x 23″ (Edition of 50)

28) *Cheep Beep.* 1974
Acrylic on acetate, 40 x 33″
Collection: Mr. and Mrs. Lawrence Aronson

29) *She Shuffled Her Eyelashes—She's a Card Shark.* 1975
Acrylic on wood, 11 x 19″
Collection: Mr. and Mrs. Terence Longo

30) *Waffle Face.* 1975
Acrylic on paper maché, 10½ x 14½″

31) *Park Alot.* 1975
Acrylic on cardboard, 20 x 37″

32) *In Memoriam for Earl 'the Mole' Seagull.* 1975
Acrylic on acetate, 26½ x 22″

33) *Rear View Mirror Watering Hole.* 1975
Acrylic on acetate, 24¾ x 22″

34) *88 Keys Revisited.* 1976
Acrylic on wood, 12¼ x 12½″

35) *Great Skates #1.* 1976
Acrylic on cardboard, 41½ x 31½″
Collection: Galerie Bonnier, Geneva

36) *Great Skates #3.* 1976
Acrylic on cardboard, 41½ x 31½″

37) *Candle Opera Phantom of Love.* 1976
Acrylic on acetate, 36 x 24″

38) *Parking Attendants Attend Dance.* 1976
Acrylic on acetate, 40 x 48″
Collection: Harold and Gayle Kurtz

39) *Hari Kari's Arms Exchange.* 1976
Acrylic on acetate, 32 x 66¾″

40) *Mr. Big Arms in a No Swipe Place* 1977
Acrylic on acetate, 28 x 23″

41) *Silk Gives Slick the Slip Before the Torch.* 1977
Acrylic on acetate, 21½ x 25″

42) *Snow Crows Tip Their Hats.* 1977
Acrylic on acetate, 21 x 20″

43) *Tin-Eared Tenor.* 1978
Acrylic on wood, 13½ x 9¼ x 3½″
Collection: Mr. and Mrs. Lawrence Aronson

44) *Ramon (Surfer)* 1978
Acrylic on wood, 21 x 17 x 10″
Collection: Roger Brown

45) *Sand Blast Exterminating Company.* 1978
Acrylic on canvas, 36 x 27″
Collection: The Museum of Contemporary Art, Chicago.

46) *Draw Dick Tracy the Hard Way.* 1978
4 offset lithographs, each 8½ x 11″

47) *Three Hulk Clone Seconds.* 1979
Acrylic on tracing paper, 20½ x 16″

48) *Any One? Ten Is!* 1979
Acrylic on wood, 30½ x 30 x 18″
Collection: Roger Brown

49) *Into Each Life a Little Rain Must Spring.* 1979
Acrylic on canvas, 36½ x 21½″
Private Collection

50) *Fits Tutu to a Tee or Stretch Your Coffee Break.* 1979
Colored pencil on paper, 41¼ x 33½″
Collection: Carol Celentano

51) *Rabbit Double Scoop Gyro with Windshields.* 1981
Acrylic on canvas, 38¾ x 28½″
Collection: Mr. and Mrs. Steven Alpert

52) *Helium Hare with Sliced Salami Necktie.* 1981
Acrylic on canvas, 36 x 24″
Collection: Lee Wesley and Victoria Granacki

53) *Redfinger Girl (Biographic Biography).* 1981
Crayon on paper, 29⅞ x 22½″
Collection: Mr. and Mrs. Douglas Cohen

54) *Eraser Eyebrows.* 1982
Acrylic and erasers on wood, 22½ x 10 x 4″

Collection: Robert A. Lewis

55)   *Phantom of Shoulder Separation State Park.*   1982
Acrylic on wood, 28 x 16 x 5½"

56)   *Italian Astronaut: Vito.*   1982
Acrylic on canvas, 42½ x 23½"

57)   *Italian Astronaut: Bonito.*   1982
Acrylic on canvas, 44½ x 24½"

58)   *Mind Your P's and Q's.*   1982
Acrylic on canvas, 43½ x 25½"

59)   *I'm a Lonely Little Petunia Tiptoeing Through an
Onion Patch.*   1982
Acrylic on canvas, 33⅜ x 25⅝"

60)   *Brown Derby Bouncer.*   1983
Acrylic on wood, 45 x 31 x 7¾"
Private Collection

61)   *Robert Bounce or Fly.*   1983
Acrylic on wood, 40 x 18¾ x 7½"

62)   *Assorted Window Silly Series:
Bunny Model .0052*   1983
Cloth, acrylic on wood, 22¾ x 7½ x ¾"

63)   *Formal Painting #1, Koranda Approaching
the Veranda.*   1983
Acrylic on canvas, 50½ x 30½"

64)   *Business Man's Launch in the Isuzo River:
Temperature 39° Fahrenheit.*   1983
Acrylic on canvas, 37¾ x 27½"

65)   *Count Fasco's Mouse Piece, Sleepy Jr. #1.*   1983
Acrylic on canvas, 33½ x 24½"

66)   *Count Fasco's Mouse Piece, Whitey Jr. #2.*   1983
Acrylic on canvas, 30½ x 25½"

67)   *Spitting Image.*   1983

Acrylic on canvas, 35½ x 28½"
Collection: Mr. and Mrs. Leonard Schiller

68)   *Gang Way Day Before To Day!*   1984
Acrylic on canvas, 48½ x 34½"

69)   *The Shadow of Your Simile:
The Soda Fountain Head Laughs It Off.*   1984
Colored pencil on paper, 34 x 26"

70)   *Fido, Ray and Me.*   1985
Colored pencil on cardboard, each 18 x 12"

71)   *Me.*   1985
Acrylic on canvas, 52½ x 36"

72)   *Double Dribble in the Ozone.*   1985
Acrylic on canvas, 52½ x 43½"

73)   *Boulevard Matador Star Grazing.*   1985
Colored pencil on paper, 50 x 38"
Collection: Mr. and Mrs. Lawrence Milner

74)   *Coma Dent.*   1985
Acrylic on acetate, 42 x 44½"

75)   *Stork Reality.*   1985
Acrylic on canvas, 32½ x 23½"

76)   *Street Steven.*   1985
Acrylic on canvas, 48½ x 35½"
Collection: Jeffrey Usow

77)   *Mr. Whatzit on the Road to Burma Shave.*   1985
Acrylic on canvas, 48¼ x 36¼"

78)   *The Arched Flip: Heads I Lose, Tails You Win.*   1986
Acrylic on canvas, 50½ x 40¼"

79)   *Hand Me Dawn Sumi.*   1986
Acrylic on canvas, 36½ x 48½"

80)   *Tuskarama Nails One Down.*   1986
Acrylic on canvas, 50½ x 36½"